Introduc

Your child's room will come to life with these adorable animal quilt blocks.

Choose fabrics like those on our bright and lively models, or pick background fabrics to match your color scheme. Either way, the cheerful smiles and cute animal poses will add color and sparkle to your home.

You can use a single block for a pillow, or to adorn a sweatshirt; use a few blocks for a wall hanging; or use all of the blocks to create a quilt.

Complete foundation-piecing instructions, along with full-color patterns, make sewing the blocks easy and fun.

Design Directory

Page 11

Page 12

Page 17

Page 30

Page 24

Page 27

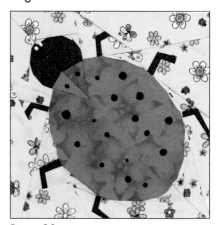

Page 29

General Directions

The Patterns

All of the blocks in this book are 7" finished. However, you may choose to enlarge one or more blocks to use for a pillow or wall hanging. Some quilters may enjoy working with larger pieces of fabric, which is another reason that you may choose to enlarge these designs.

The full-color patterns have more than one section that must be foundation-pieced individually, and then sewn together. Bold lines that are also the cutting lines indicate these sections. A piecing diagram is included with each block showing the piecing order of the sections.

Also included with each block pattern is a photograph showing the completed block. Note the asymetrical blocks become mirror images of the original patterns, **Fig 1**.

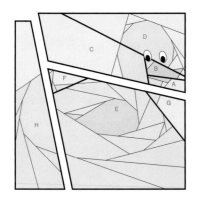

Fig 1

Fabric

We recommend using 100-percent cotton fabric for piecing. By using cotton rather than cotton/polyester blends, the pieces will not slip as easily and they will respond better to finger-pressing.

Prewashing fabric is not necessary, but it is advisable to test your fabric to make certain that the fabric is colorfast. Place a 2"-wide strip (cut crosswise) of fabric into a bowl of extremely hot water; if the water changes color, the fabric is bleeding and it will be necessary to wash that fabric until all of the excess dye has washed out. Repeat for all fabrics that will be used for your quilt. Fabrics that continue to bleed after they have been washed several times should be eliminated.

To test for shrinkage, take each saturated strip (used above in the colorfast test) and iron it dry with a hot iron. When the strip is completely dry, measure and compare it to your original 2" measurement. If all of your strips shrink about the same amount, then you really have no problem. When you wash your quilt, you may achieve the puckered look of an antique quilt. If you do not want this look, you will have to wash and dry all fabric before beginning so that shrinkage is no longer an issue. If any of your test strips are shrinking more than the others, these fabrics will need to be prewashed and dried, or discarded.

Embellishments

Many of the blocks have been enhanced with embellishments such as buttons, beads, felt appliqués and marker-drawn features.

Safety Note: *To eliminate the chance of a child's choking, do NOT use buttons, beads or small glued items on any quilt that will be handled by small children!*

In addition to items listed with the projects, you will find the following supplies helpful for embellishing your swatches:

Glue
Permanent fabric-marking pens
Coordinating sewing thread

The Foundation-Piecing Method

Foundation Material

Before you start sewing, you need to decide the type of foundation on which to piece your blocks. There are several options. Paper is a popular choice for machine piecing because it is readily available and inexpensive. Copier paper works well, but newsprint found in office supply stores is much easier to handle since it is not as stiff. The paper is removed after the blocks are completely sewn.

Another alternative for foundation piecing is muslin or cotton fabric that is lightweight and light-color for easy tracing. The fabric will add another layer that you will have to quilt through, but that is only a consideration if you are going to hand quilt. Also, if you use a fabric foundation, you will be able to hand piece your blocks if that is your desire.

A third option for foundation material is Tear Away or Fun-dation™ translucent nonwoven material. Like muslin, it is light enough to see through for tracing, but like paper, it can be easily removed before quilting.

A new type of "disappearing" foundation material by W.H. Collins is called WashAway™ foundation paper. After sewing, place block in water and the foundation dissolves in 10 seconds.

Preparing the Foundation
Tracing the Block

Trace the block pattern carefully onto your chosen foundation material. Use a ruler and a fine-point permanent marker or fine-line mechanical pencil to make straight lines; be sure to include all numbers and letters for multiple sections. Repeat for the number of blocks needed for your quilt.

Cutting the Fabric

One of biggest advantages to foundation piecing is that you do not have to cut exact pieces for every block. This is especially important for smaller blocks or blocks with many small pieces. It is much easier to handle a small section or strip of fabric than it is to handle a triangle where the finished size of the sides is ¼".

The main consideration for using fabric pieces for a particular space is that the fabric must be at least ¼" larger on all sides than the space it is to cover. Squares and strips are easy to figure, but triangle shapes can be a little tricky to piece. Use generous-size fabric pieces and be careful when positioning the pieces onto the foundation. You do waste some fabric this way, but the time it saves in cutting will be worth it in the end.

*Hint: Measure the width of a particular space on your pattern; add ½" and cut a strip to that width, **Fig 2.** You will save time since you won't have to trim each seam allowance as you go.*

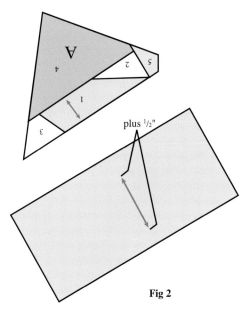

plus ½"

Fig 2

How to Make a Foundation-Pieced Block

1. Prepare foundations as described in Preparing the Foundation, marking the letter and number of each section as shown on the pattern. Cut foundations apart along the bold lines to separate pattern into smaller sections, **Fig 3.**

Fig 3

2. Starting with section A, turn foundation section with unmarked side facing you and position piece 1 right side up over the space marked "1" on the foundation. Hold foundation up to a light source to make sure that fabric overlaps at least ¼" on all sides of space 1, **Fig 4.** Pin or use a glue stick to hold fabric in place.

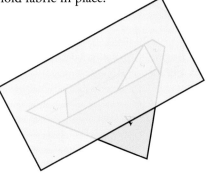

Fig 4

Note: *Use only a small amount of a fresh glue stick to hold fabric in place. It is especially helpful to use a glue stick to keep larger or narrow pieces in place on the foundation until the blocks are sewn together.*

3. Turn foundation over. With marked side of foundation facing you, fold foundation forward along line between space 1 and 2 and trim fabric about ¼" from fold if needed, **Fig 5.**

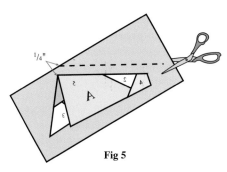

Fig 5

4. Place fabric piece 2 right sides together with piece 1; edge of fabric 2 should be even with just-trimmed edge of fabric 1, **Fig 6.** Double-check to see if fabric piece chosen will cover space 2 completely by folding over along line between space 1 and 2, **Fig 7.**

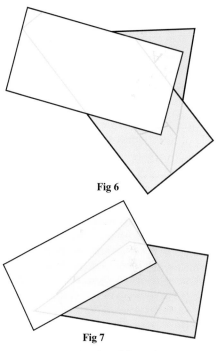

Fig 6

Fig 7

5. With marked side of foundation facing you, place on sewing machine, holding fabric pieces together. Sew along line between spaces 1 and 2 using a very small stitch (18–20 stitches per inch), **Fig 8.** Begin and end sewing two to three stitches beyond line. You do not need to backstitch.

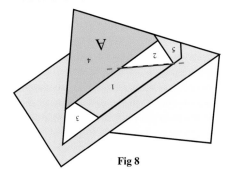

Fig 8

Hint: *Sewing with very tiny stitches will allow for easier paper removal later. If paper falls apart after stitching, your stitch length is too small, and you will need to lengthen the stitch slightly.*

6. Turn foundation over. Open piece 2 and finger-press seam, **Fig 9**. Use a pin or dab of glue stick to hold piece in place if necessary.

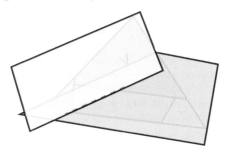

Fig 9

Hint: *If using strips, trim extra length, being sure to leave enough to cover entire area plus seam allowance.*

7. Turn foundation with marked side of foundation facing you; fold foundation forward along line between spaces 1 and 3 and trim ¼" from fold if necessary, **Fig 10**. *Note: If you have used a premeasured strip as described in Cutting the Fabric, you will not need to do this step.*

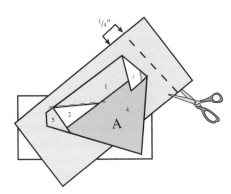

Fig 10

8. Place fabric 3 right side down, even with just-trimmed edge, **Fig 11**.

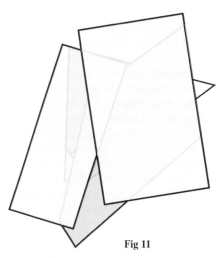

Fig 11

9. Turn foundation to marked side and sew along line between spaces 1 and 3; begin and end sewing two to three stitches beyond line, **Fig 12**.

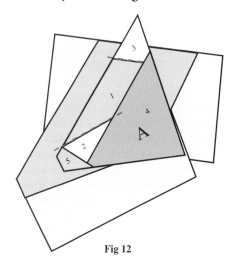

Fig 12

10. Turn foundation over, open piece 3 and finger-press seam. Glue or pin in place, **Fig 13**.

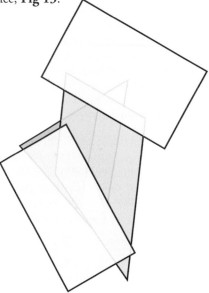

Fig 13

11. Turn foundation with marked side facing you. Fold foundation forward along line between spaces 2 and 4; trim fabrics 1, 2 and 3 to about ¼" away from fold, **Fig 14**.

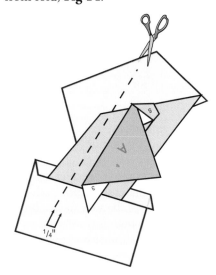

Fig 14

Hint: *If using a paper foundation, carefully pull paper away from stitching for easier trimming. If using a fabric foundation, fold it forward as far as it will go and trim.*

12. Continue trimming and sewing pieces in numerical order until section is complete, **Fig 15**. Make sure pieces along the outer edge are large enough to allow for the ¼" seam allowance.

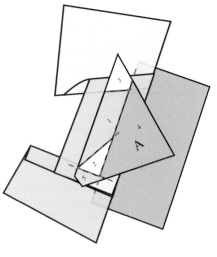

Fig 15

13. Press, then trim fabric ¼" from outside line of foundation to complete section, **Fig 16**.

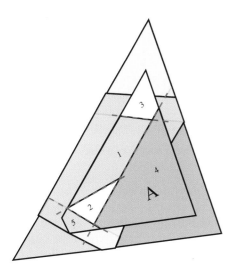

Fig 16

14. Complete remaining sections of block in same manner.

15. Study the piecing diagram found on the pattern page. Sew sections in alphabetical order.

Note: For some patterns, you may have to piece small sections before sewing to a previous section. For example, Kitty Face, page 13, has sections A to H. Sew A to B and C to D, then sew these units to E. Sew F to this unit. Sew G and H to this unit to complete the block.

To sew sections, place right sides together; push a pin through corner of top section going through to corner of bottom section. Check to be sure pin goes through both corners and is perpendicular (going straight up) to section, **Fig 17**. If not, pin again until corners match.

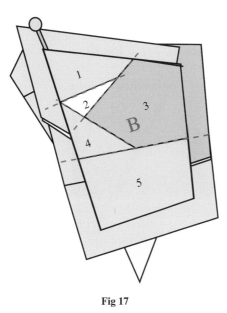

Fig 17

Repeat at opposite end of seam line to match corners. It is also a good idea to pin the intersections of seams that should line up between the two sections, **Fig 18**.

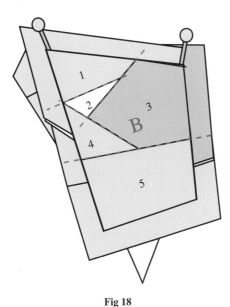

Fig 18

Hint: If desired, baste sections together by hand or machine. Check sections again; if everything matches up, sew together with regular stitches. Basting takes a little time, but the extra effort will be worth it in the end.

16. Once pieces are lined up correctly, sew along edge of foundation using a regular stitch length, **Fig 19**.

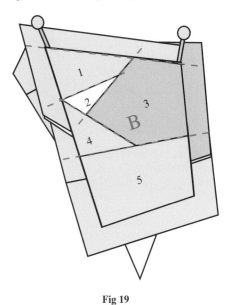

Fig 19

17. Sew remaining sections together, referring to the order in the piecing diagram with each pattern.

*Hint: Do not remove paper yet. It is better to remove paper after blocks have been sewn together. Since grainline was not considered in piecing, outer edges may be on the bias and, therefore, stretchy. Keeping paper in place until after sewing will prevent the blocks from becoming distorted. Staystitching along outer edge of block, **Fig 20**, will also help keep fabric from stretching out of shape.*

Fig 20

Highlights & Hints for Foundation Piecing

• Begin and end sewing at least two to three stitches beyond line you are sewing, **Fig 21**.

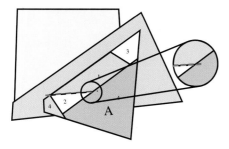

Fig 21

• Don't worry if your stitching goes through a whole space and into another space, **Fig 22**; it will not interfere with adding subsequent pieces.

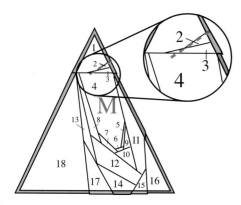

Fig 22

• Finger-press or press with an iron after every seam. The little wooden "irons" found in quilt shops or catalogs work great.

• Use a short stitch, around 20 stitches per inch.

• Trim seam allowances to ⅛"–¼" (or smaller if necessary for small sections).

• Don't worry too much about grainline. Sewing to a foundation stabilizes the fabric and will prevent it from getting out of shape.

• When sewing spaces with points, it is easier to start sewing from the wide end towards the point, **Fig 23**.

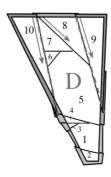

Fig 23

• Directional prints are not recommended unless they are used only once in a block or are placed where they can be used easily in a consistent manner. If directional prints are placed randomly, the effect in the finished block may be undesirable.

Finishing the Quilt

Making the Quilt Top

Make the number of blocks necessary for your quilt top.

Lay out blocks in desired arrangement. Sew quilt blocks together in rows; press seams for rows in alternate directions. Sew rows together, matching seams.

To add borders, measure quilt top lengthwise; cut two border strips to that length and sew to sides of quilt. Measure quilt top crosswise, including borders just added; cut two border strips to that length. Sew to top and bottom edges of quilt top. Repeat for any additional borders.

Layering the Quilt

There are many types of batting on the market. Use batting that is suitable for the use of your quilt. If making a wall hanging, choose a thin cotton or polyester batting. If making a bed quilt, you may want low-loft polyester batting for a little more thickness. Check the label to see the quilting requirements and follow those guidelines.

Use 100-percent cotton fabric for the backing of your quilt. For quilts wider than the 40"–44"-wide fabric, you will have to piece your backing unless you use the 90"–106"-wide fabrics that are currently available.

Cut backing and batting about 1"–2" larger on all sides than the quilt top. Place backing wrong side up, then smooth out batting on top. Center quilt top right side up on batting.

Baste layers together using one of the following techniques:

Fusible iron-on batting—The new Fusible Batting™ by June Tailor, and Gold-Fuse by Mountain Mist® are wonderful new ways to hold the quilt layers together without using other time-consuming methods of basting.

Thread basting—Baste with long stitches, starting in center and sewing toward edges in a number of diagonal lines.

Safety-pin basting—Pin through all layers at once, starting from center and working toward edges. Place pins no more than 4" apart, thinking of your quilt plan as you work to make certain pins avoid prospective quilting lines.

Quilt-gun basting—Use the handy trigger tool (found in quilt and fabric stores) that pushes nylon tags through all layers of the quilt. Start in center and work randomly toward outside edges. Place tags about 4" apart. You can sew right over the tags and then easily remove them by cutting off with a pair of scissors.

Spray or heat-set basting—Use one of the spray adhesives currently on the market, following manufacturer's directions.

Quilting

If you have never used a sewing machine for quilting, you might want to read more about the technique. *Learn to Machine Quilt in Just One Weekend* (ASN #4186), by Marti Michell, is an excellent introduction to machine quilting. This book is available at your local quilt or fabric store, or write the publisher for a list of sources.

You do not need a special machine for quilting. Just make sure your machine is oiled and in good working condition. An even-feed foot is a good investment if you are going to machine quilt, since it is designed to feed the top and bottom layers of the quilt through the machine evenly. Use fine transparent nylon thread in the top and regular sewing thread in the bobbin.

To quilt in the ditch of a seam (this is actually stitching in the space between two pieces of fabric that have been sewn together), use your fingers to pull blocks or pieces apart slightly and machine-stitch right between the two pieces. Try to keep stitching to the side of the seam that does not have the bulk of the seam allowance under it. When you have finished stitching, the quilting will be practically hidden in the seam.

Free-form machine quilting is done with a darning foot and the feed dogs down on your sewing machine. It can be used to quilt around a design or to quilt a motif. Free-form machine quilting takes practice to master because you are controlling the movement of the quilt under the needle, rather than the machine moving the quilt. With free-form machine quilting, you can quilt in any direction: up and down, side to side and even in circles, without pivoting the quilt around the needle.

Attaching the Binding

Trim backing and batting even with quilt top. Cut enough 2½"-wide strips to go around all four sides of quilt, plus 6". Join strips end to end with diagonal seams; trim corners, **Fig 24**.

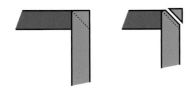

Fig 24

Press seams open. Cut one end of strip at a 45-degree angle, then press under ¼", **Fig 25**.

Fig 25

Press entire strip in half lengthwise, wrong sides together, **Fig 26**.

Fig 26

On right side of quilt, position binding in middle of one side, aligning raw edges. Sew binding to quilt using ¼" seam, beginning about an inch below folded end of binding, **Fig 27**.

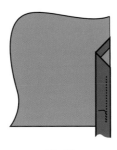

Fig 27

At corner, stop ¼" from edge of quilt and backstitch. Fold binding away from quilt at a 45-degree angle. Fold binding back on itself so fold is on quilt edge and raw edges are aligned with adjacent side of quilt, **Fig 28**. Begin sewing at quilt edge.

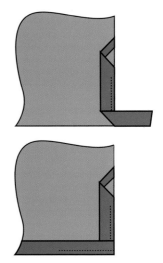

Fig 28

Continue in the same manner around remaining sides of quilt. To finish, stop about 2" away from starting point. Trim excess binding, then tuck inside folded end, **Fig 29**. Finish line of stitching.

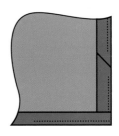

Fig 29

Fold binding to back of quilt so seam line is covered; blindstitch in place.

The Finishing Touch

After your quilt is finished, always sign and date it. A label can be cross-stitched, embroidered or even written with a permanent marking pen. To make decorative labels in a hurry, *Iron-on Transfers for Quilt Labels* (ASN #4188) and *Foundation-Pieced Quilt Labels* (ASN #4196), provide many patterns for fun and unique quilt labels. Hand stitch to back of quilt.

Bunny

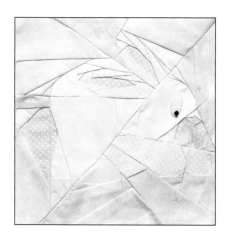

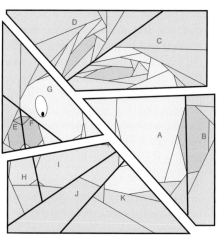

Special notes:

Trace eye oval from design pattern onto piece of white felt. Referring to design pattern, attach felt piece and sew on 4mm black glass bead for eye.

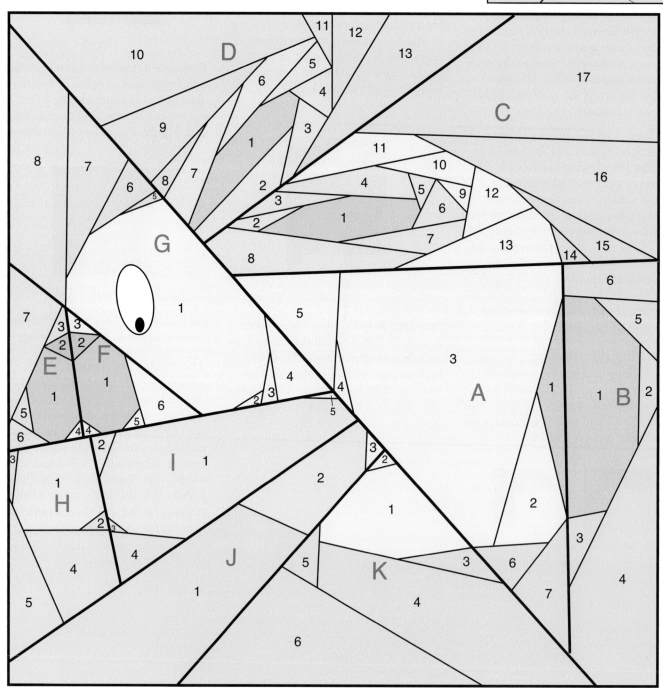

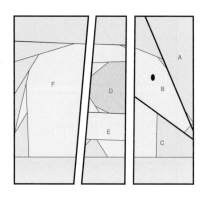

Elephant

Special notes:

Referring to design pattern, draw eye with black fabric-marking pen.

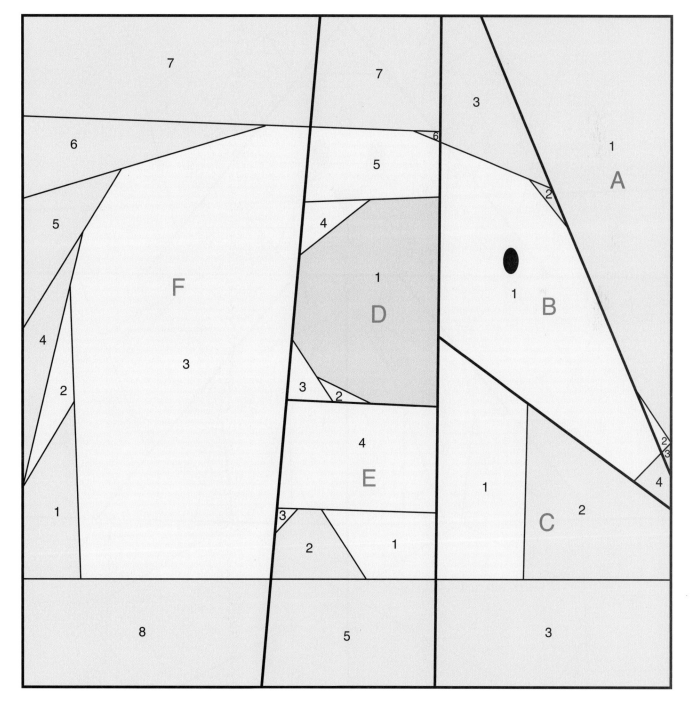

Teddy Bear

Special notes:

Referring to design pattern, draw eyes, nose and mouth with black fabric-marking pen.

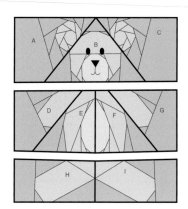

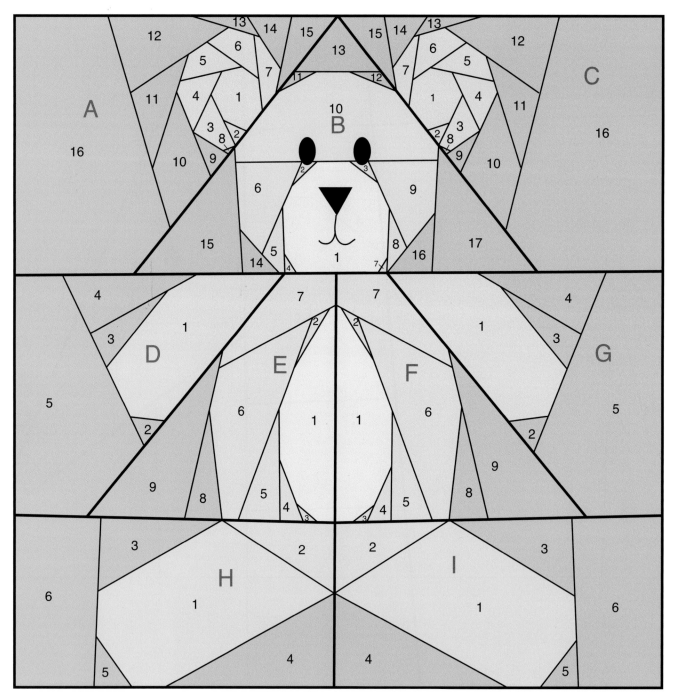

Teddy Bear Face

Special notes:

Trace eyes, nose and mouth from design pattern onto black felt. Referring to design pattern, attach felt pieces. Draw mouth lines with black fabric-marking pen.

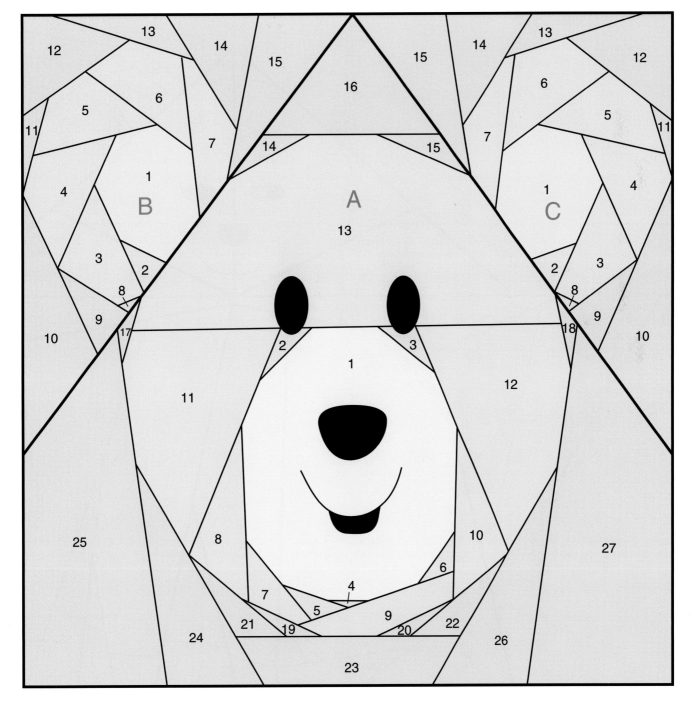

Kitty

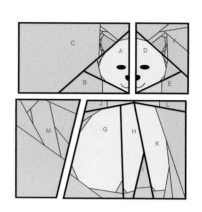

Special notes:

Referring to design pattern, draw eyes, nose and mouth with black fabric-marking pen.

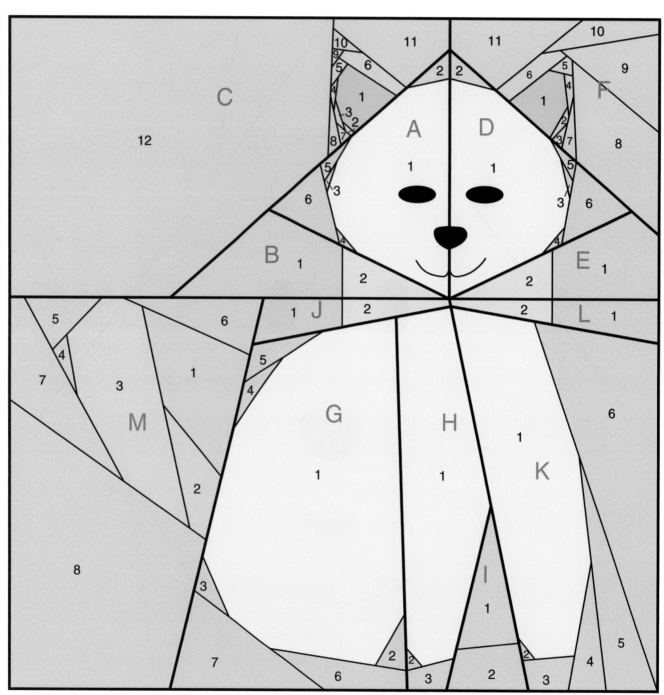

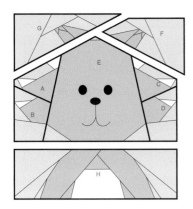

Kitty Face

Special notes:

Trace nose from design pattern onto piece of black felt. Referring to design pattern, attach felt for nose and two ½" black shank buttons for eyes. Draw mouth with black fabric-marking pen.

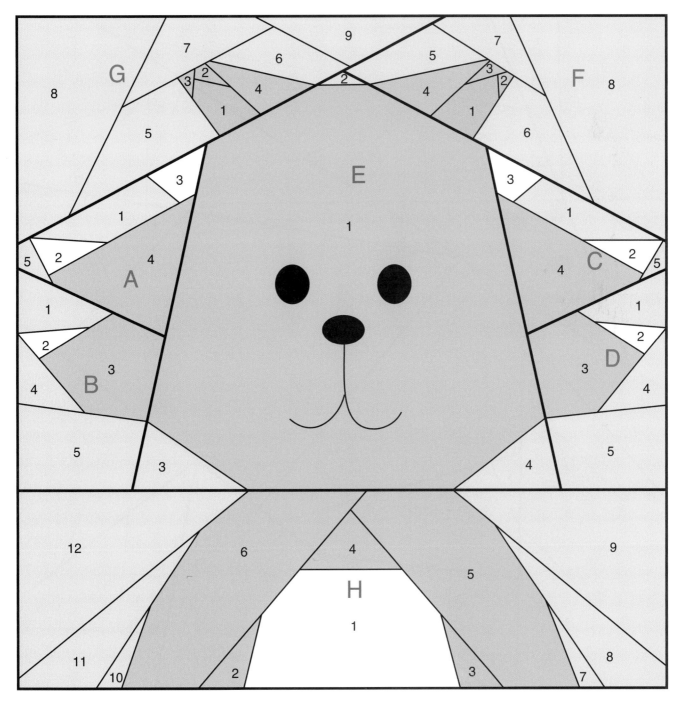

Puppy

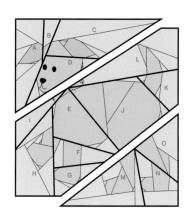

Special notes:

Referring to design pattern, draw eyes, nose and mouth with black fabric-marking pen.

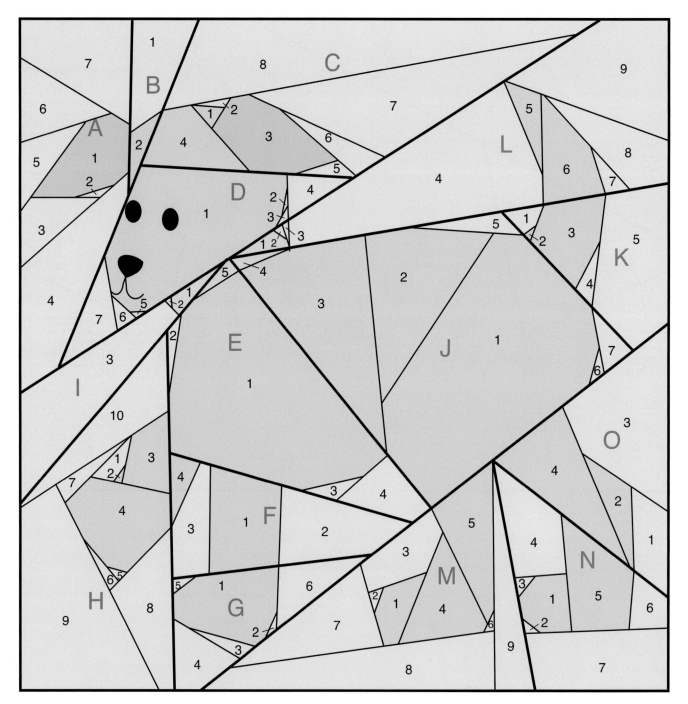

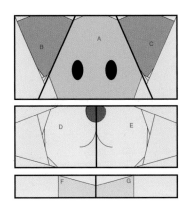

Puppy Face

Special notes:

Trace eye ovals and nose shape from design pattern onto black felt. Referring to design pattern, attach felt eyes and nose and draw mouth with black fabric-marking pen.

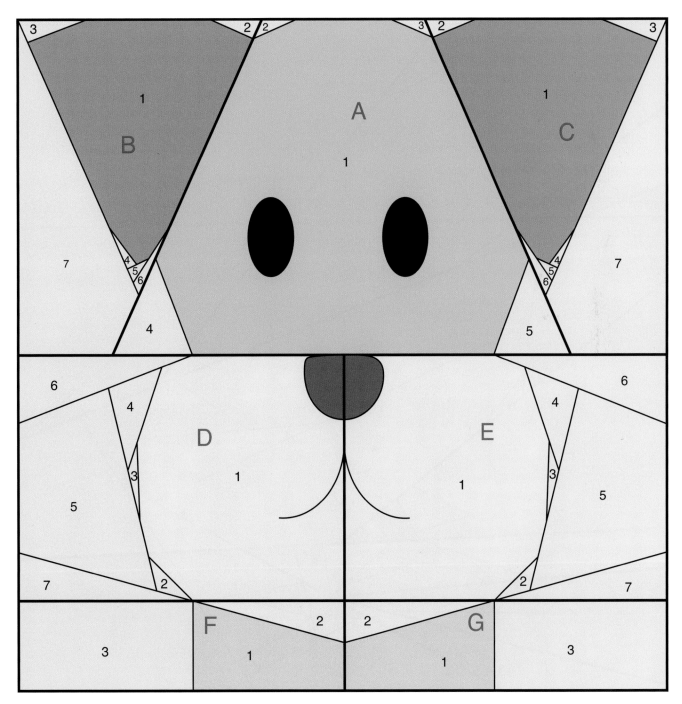

Baby Chick

Special notes:

Referring to design pattern, attach ⅜" black shank button for eye.

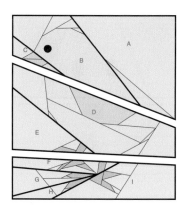

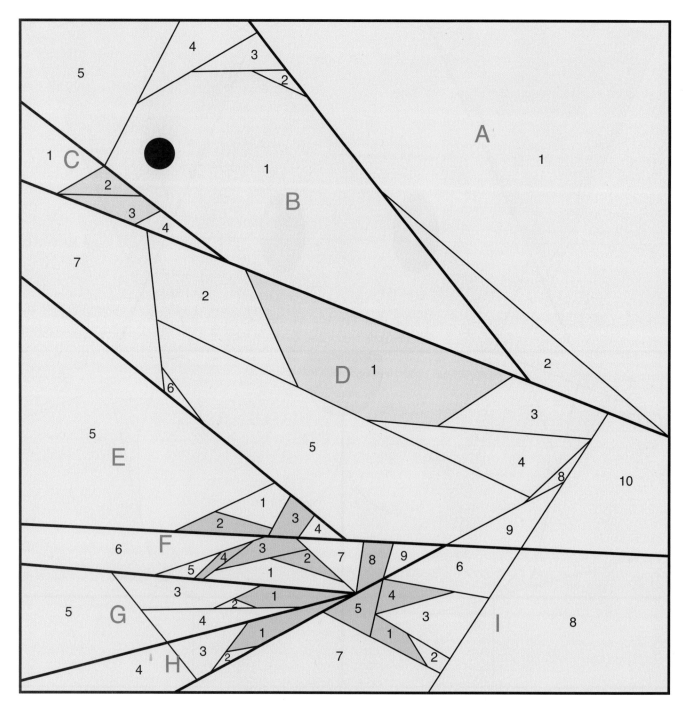

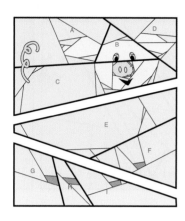

Piglet

Special notes:

Referring to design pattern, draw eyes, nose and mouth with black fabric-marking pen. Attach curly tail using 6" (¼"-wide) pink cord.

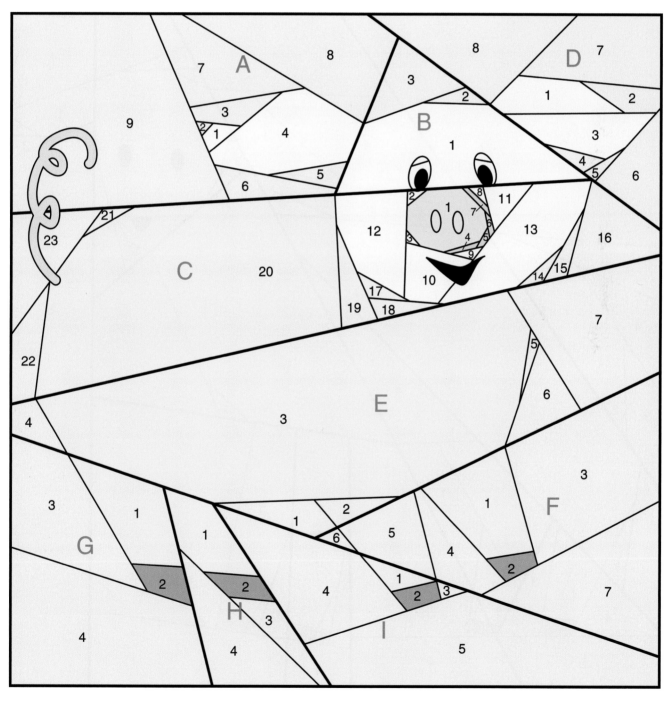

Lamb

Special notes:

Referring to design pattern, draw eyes and nose with black fabric-marking pen.

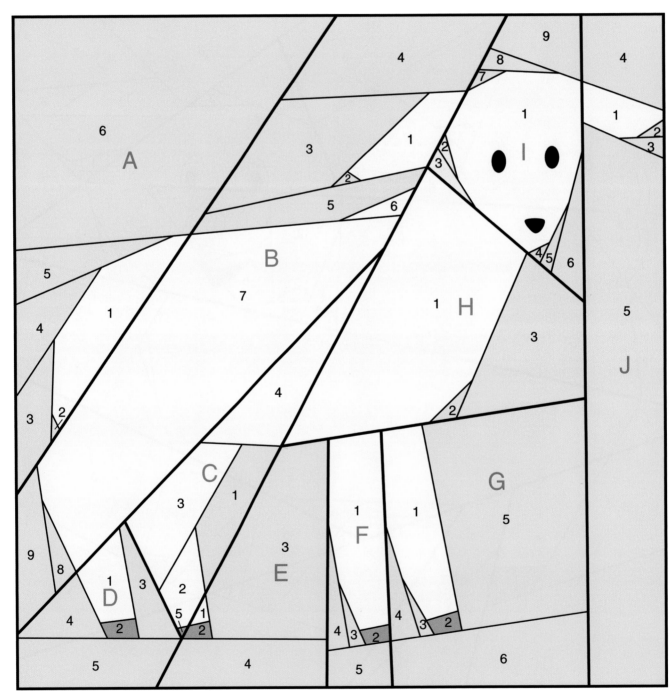

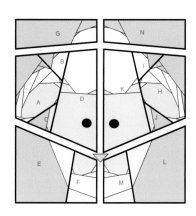

Lamb Face

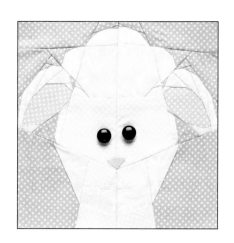

Special notes:

Trace nose from design pattern onto piece of pink felt. Referring to design pattern, attach felt piece and sew on two ½" black shank buttons for eyes.

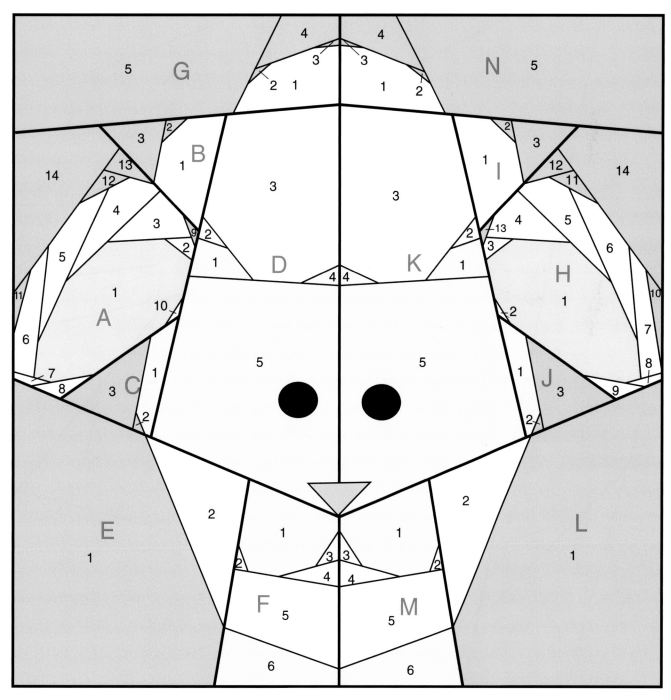

Ducky

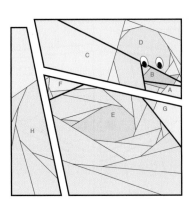

Special notes:

Trace eye ovals from design pattern onto white felt.
Referring to design pattern, attach felt pieces and
sew on two 4mm black glass beads for eyes.

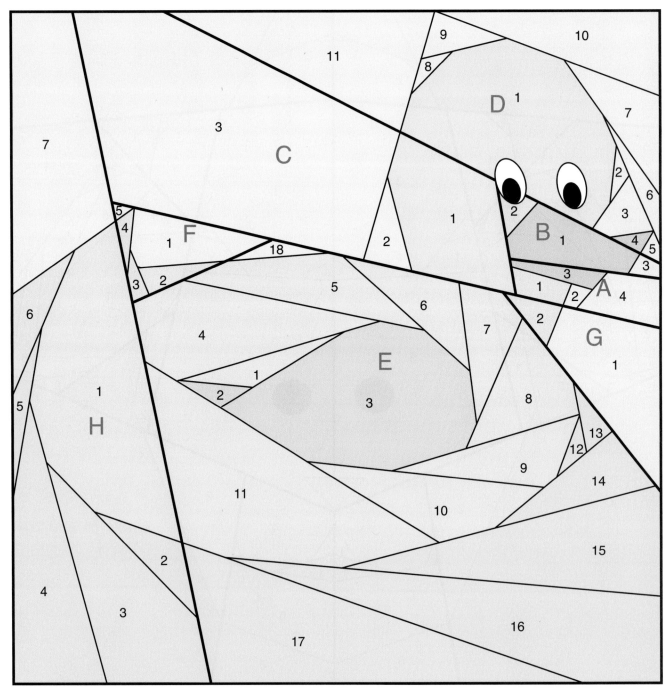

Pony

Special notes:

Referring to design pattern, draw eye with black fabric-marking pen.

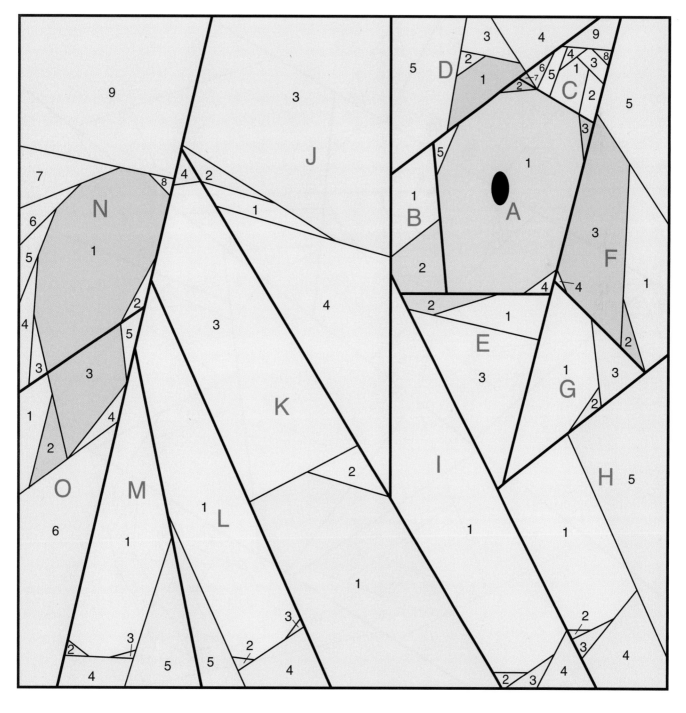

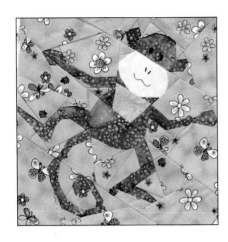

Monkey

Special notes:

Referring to design pattern, draw eyes, nose and mouth with black fabric-marking pen.

Giraffe

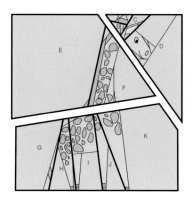

Special notes:

Referring to design pattern, draw eye, nose and mouth with black fabric-marking pen. Draw spots with brown fabric-marking pen.

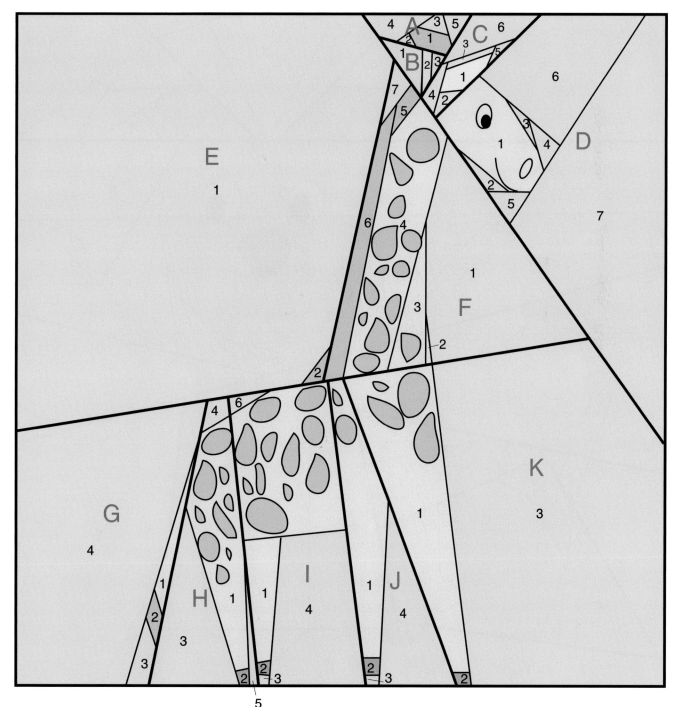

Lion

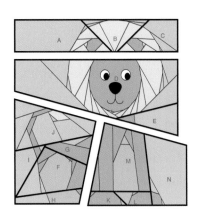

Special notes:

Trace eye ovals from design pattern onto white felt and nose shape onto black felt. Referring to design pattern, attach felt eyes and nose, and add two ¼ " black faceted beads for eyes. Draw mouth with black fabric-marking pen.

Panda

Special notes:

Trace eyes and nose from design pattern onto black felt. Referring to design pattern, attach felt eyes and nose and add two 4mm white beads for eyes. Draw mouth with black fabric-marking pen.

Dinosaur Baby

Special notes:

Trace eyes from design pattern onto white felt. Referring to design pattern, attach felt pieces and two 4mm black beads for eyes. Draw mouth with black fabric-marking pen.

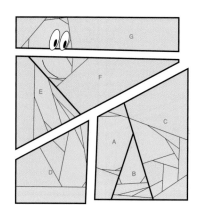

Dinosaur

Special notes:

Trace eyes from design pattern onto white felt. Referring to design pattern, attach felt pieces and two 4mm black beads for eyes. Draw mouth with black fabric-marking pen.

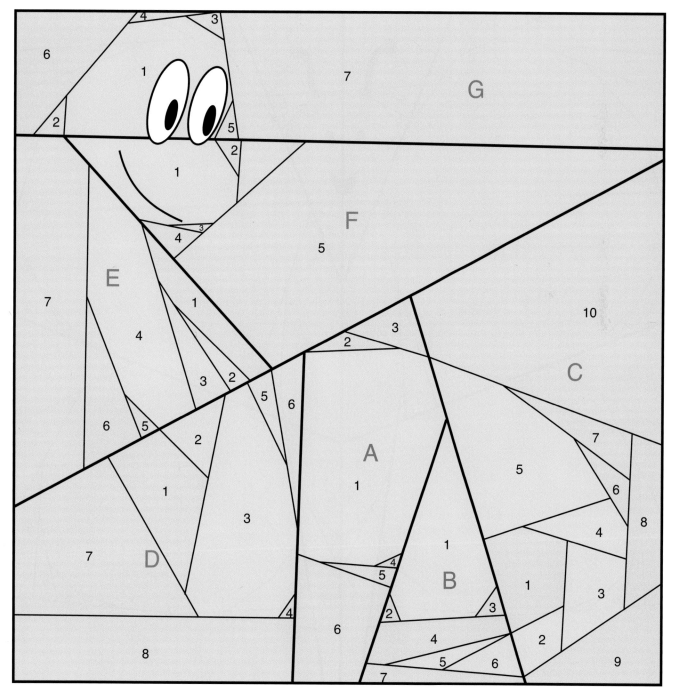

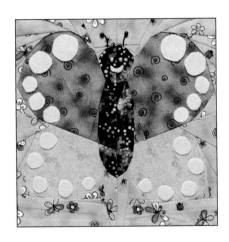

Butterfly

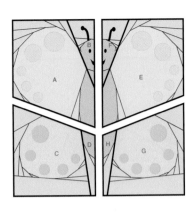

Special notes:

Trace mouth from design pattern onto light blue felt. Trace spots on upper wings onto pink felt and spots on lower wings onto light blue felt. Referring to design pattern, attach felt mouth and spots. Attach two 4mm light blue beads for eyes. Draw antennae with black fabric-marking pen, and attach two (4mm) black beads at tips of antennae.

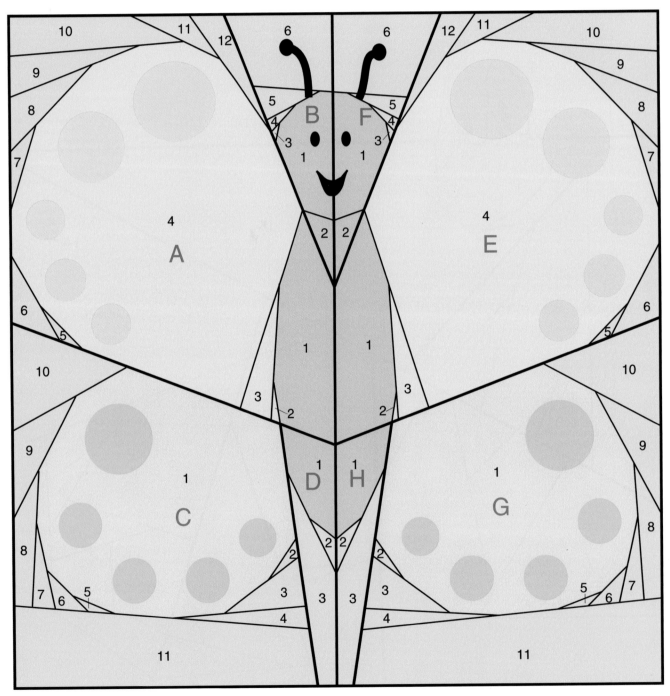

Ladybug

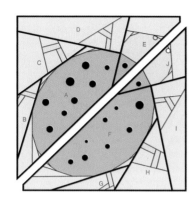

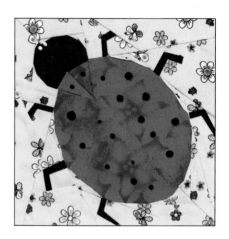

Special notes:

Attach two 4mm white beads for eyes. Draw spots on ladybug's back with black fabric-marking pen.

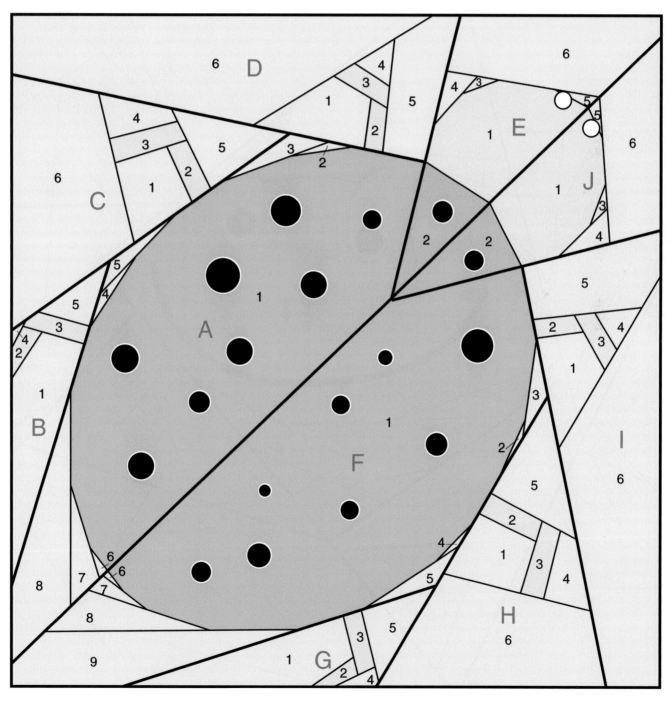

Frog

Special notes:

Trace eye ovals from design pattern onto white felt. Referring to design pattern, attach felt eyes and attach two ⅜" black shank buttons. Draw nose and mouth with black fabric-marking pen.

Turtle

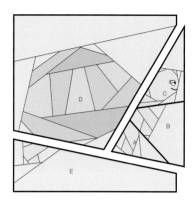

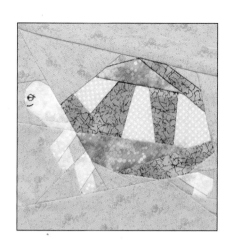

Special notes:

Referring to design pattern, draw eye and mouth with black fabric-marking pen.

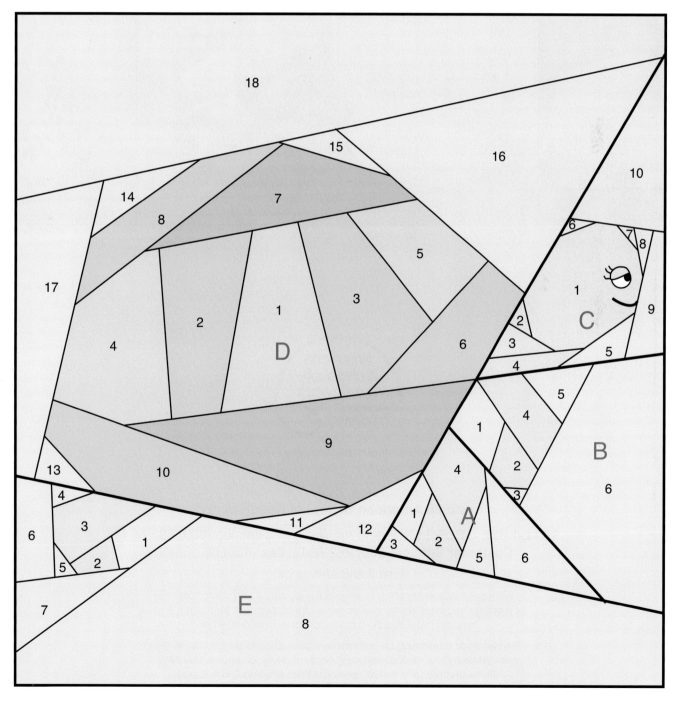

Thanks to Northcott Silk Inc., for providing cotton fabrics for these projects.

www.northcott.net

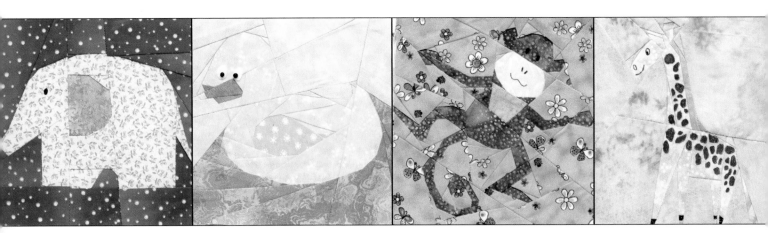

American School of Needlework®
excellence in instruction

DRG Publishing
306 East Parr Road
Berne, IN 46711
©2005 American School of Needlework

TOLL-FREE ORDER LINE or to request a free catalog (800) 582-6643
Customer Service (800) 282-6643, **Fax** (800) 882-6643
Visit AnniesAttic.com.